W9-CEK-160

ANIMAL SUPERPOWERS

SALAMANDER

JOSH PLATTNER

CONSULTING EDITOR, DIANE CRAIG, M.A./READING SPECIALIST

Super Sandcastle

An Imprint of Abdo Publishing
abdopublishing.com

abdopublishing.com

Published by Abdo Publishing, a division of ABDO, PO Box 398166, Minneapolis, Minnesota 55439. Copyright © 2016 by Abdo Consulting Group, Inc. International copyrights reserved in all countries. No part of this book may be reproduced in any form without written permission from the publisher. Super SandCastle™ is a trademark and logo of Abdo Publishing.

Printed in the United States of America, North Mankato, Minnesota
062015
092015

THIS BOOK CONTAINS RECYCLED MATERIALS

Editor: Liz Salzmann
Content Developer: Nancy Tuminelly
Cover and Interior Design and Production: Anders Hanson, Mighty Media, Inc.
Photo Credits: Shutterstock

Library of Congress Cataloging-in-Publication Data
Plattner, Josh, author.
  Salamander : master of regrowth / Josh Plattner ; consulting editor, Diane Craig, M.A./reading specialist.
      pages cm. -- (Animal superpowers)
  Audience: K to grade 4
  ISBN 978-1-62403-740-5
1. Salamanders--Juvenile literature. I. Title.
  QL668.C2P53 2016
  597.8'5--dc23
                    2014048275

Super SandCastle™ books are created by a team of professional educators, reading specialists, and content developers around five essential components— phonemic awareness, phonics, vocabulary, text comprehension, and fluency—to assist young readers as they develop reading skills and strategies and increase their general knowledge. All books are written, reviewed, and leveled for guided reading, early reading intervention, and Accelerated Reader™ programs for use in shared, guided, and independent reading and writing activities to support a balanced approach to literacy instruction.

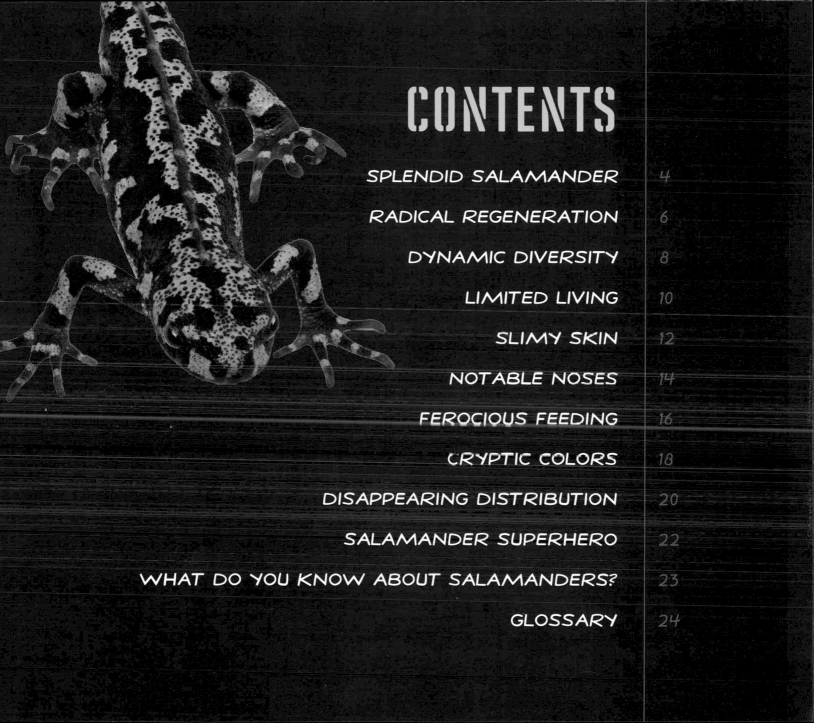

CONTENTS

SPLENDID SALAMANDER

Salamanders are amphibians. There are more than 650 **species**. They look like lizards.

They have short limbs. Most salamanders have long tails.

RADICAL
REGENERATION

What is this animal's superpower? **Regeneration**! When a salamander loses its tail, it grows back. Salamanders can regenerate their legs too. It only takes a few weeks!

DYNAMIC DIVERSITY

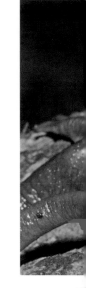

Salamanders come in many shapes. They can have different numbers of toes. Some don't have hind legs. Some have gills. Their eyes can be large. Others have flat features.

LIMITED LIVING

Many salamanders live in the northeast United States.
One third of them live on mountains.

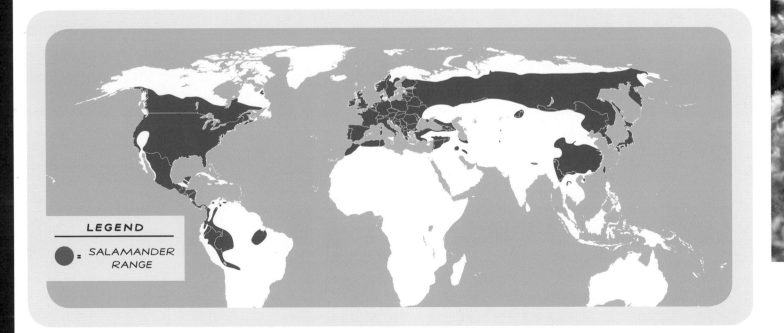

LEGEND

● = SALAMANDER RANGE

Salamanders like cooler temperatures. They prefer wet climates.

SLIMY SKIN

Salamander skin is **permeable**. This means liquids can pass through it.

Mucus keeps their skin moist. It allows them to breathe in water.

NOTABLE NOSES

Salamanders
have a great
sense of smell.
Their scents
attract mates.

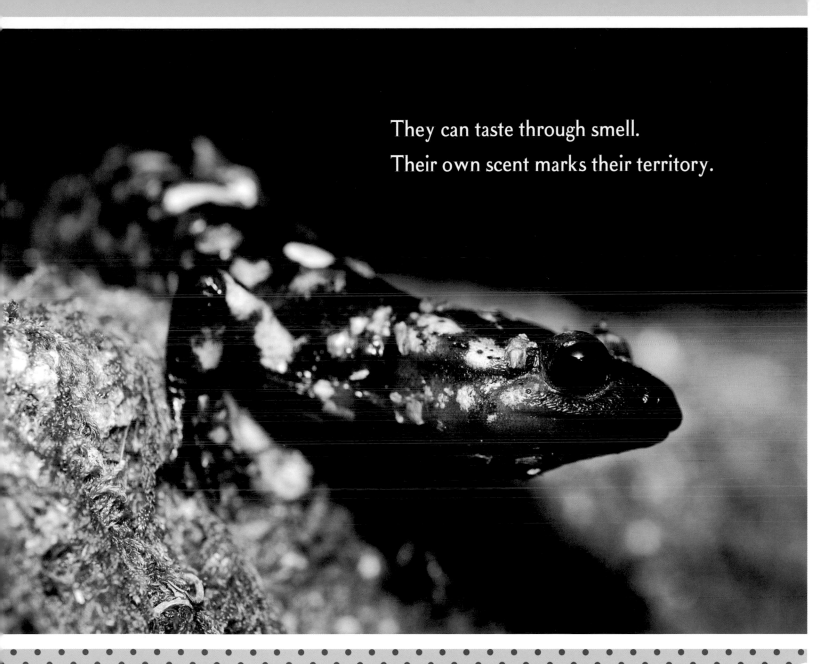

They can taste through smell.

Their own scent marks their territory.

FEROCIOUS FEEDING

Some salamanders have long tongues. They use them to pull in **prey**.

Others have small teeth. These teeth are sharp.
Their teeth help them eat small insects.

CRYPTIC COLORS

Salamanders can be many different colors. Some **blend** in with their **habitats**. Others have bright markings.

DEADLY COLORS

Red, yellow, and orange are the most common colors.
These colors warn predators that a salamander is toxic.

DISAPPEARING
DISTRIBUTION

Many salamander **species** have become **endangered**. **Disease** is a major cause. Another cause is **habitat** loss.

Some **species** are hunted. In China, giant salamanders are killed to make medicines.

SALAMANDER SUPERHERO

Can you imagine
a salamander
superhero?
What would
it look like?
What could
it do?

WHAT DO YOU KNOW ABOUT
SALAMANDERS?

1. A salamander's superpower is jumping. *TRUE OR FALSE?*

2. It takes a few months for a salamander to **regenerate** a leg. *TRUE OR FALSE?*

3. Salamanders all look the same. *TRUE OR FALSE?*

4. Some salamanders have long tongues. *TRUE OR FALSE?*

ANSWERS:
1. FALSE   2. FALSE   3. FALSE   4. TRUE

23

GLOSSARY

ATTRACT - to cause someone or something to come near.

BLEND - to match the surrounding environment.

DISEASE - a sickness.

ENDANGERED - having few left in the world.

HABITAT - the area or environment where a person or animal usually lives.

MUCUS - a slippery, sticky substance produced by the body.

PERMEABLE - having tiny holes that let liquid or air to pass through.

PREY - an animal that is hunted or caught for food.

REGENERATE - to grow back.

SPECIES - a group of related living beings.